JANETTE OKE'S

Reflections on the

CHRISTMAS STORY

JANETTE OKE'S

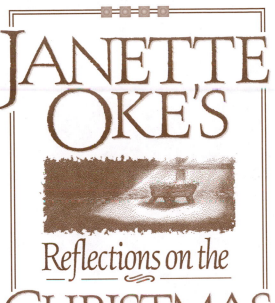

Reflections on the

CHRISTMAS STORY

BETHANY HOUSE PUBLISHERS
MINNEAPOLIS, MINNESOTA 55438

Contents

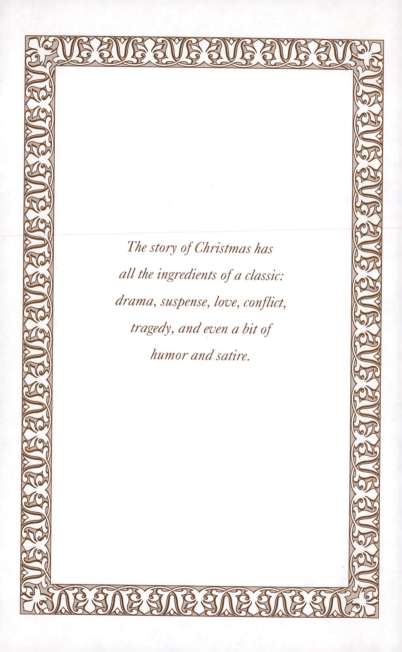

*The story of Christmas has
all the ingredients of a classic:
drama, suspense, love, conflict,
tragedy, and even a bit of
humor and satire.*

HE COULD HAVE COME

He could have come majestically—in splendor,
Shimm'ring angels proclaiming the world 'round,
Behold—the King of Heav'n is now approaching—
With Light and Power and Life, the King is crowned.

The trumpets could have signaled His appearing,
The sound of shouts and cannon blasts proclaimed,
The King had come to set to right creation,
The King of Kings—throughout the whole world
  famed.

His chariots could have been of flaming fire,
His garb of wrought gold set with burning jewels,
Upon His brow a crown to awe all people,
His pomp sufficing to declare—"He rules."

But no—He came as Bethlehem's baby,
A tiny, helpless innocent that lay

7

Within a cradle crude—'twas but a manger,
Dependent on humanity to stay

Close by, that He might live yet longer;
Given to the world to cherish—or to shame,
He could not e'en request His simple wishes,
Far less demand the honor due His name.

His guardian—a simple, lowly maiden,
A teen. No knowledge in the art
Of baby care. Far less in handling royalty.
Yet God chose her to carry out the part

Of Jesus' mother. Tender, yielded, open
Yet so alone—and oh, so far away,
She bore her son and wrapped him in the swathings
Of swaddling clothes, then placed Him on the hay.

And Joseph paced alone out in the darkness
And prayed his simple prayer yet once again—

For safe delivery of the child in nearby stable—
The woman, his wife—yet not—be freed from pain.

Only the shepherds heard the angel chorus
Announce the birth—the alleluias ring.
Only a few came to the lowly manger,
Though so few knew—this Babe was born the King.

—JANETTE OKE

THE PLOT

Plot

The interconnected series of actions through which the characters move by the will of the writer. Usually the plot involves a problem and takes the characters through the conflict toward an agreeable solution. Each part of the action moves the story one step forward toward the climax or turning point.

Fictional stories can be exciting adventures that also teach spiritual truths. When a story is factual, it carries an added dimension. The reader no longer imagines what it might have been like for the protagonist but realizes that the pain suffered, the joy expressed, and the feelings experienced all were real.

Forasmuch as many have taken in hand to set forth in order a declaration of those things which are most surely believed among us, even as they delivered them unto us, which from the beginning were eyewitnesses, and ministers of the word; it seemed good to me also, having had perfect understanding of all things from the very first, to write unto thee in order, most excellent Theophilus, that thou mightest know the certainty of those things, wherein thou hast been instructed.

LUKE 1:1-4

THE PLOT OF THE CHRISTMAS story is simple, yet complex, with subplots and interweaving events. Humanly speaking, the story is of a man and his commitment—a commitment so strong that it overcame the evidence of infidelity.

There is a journey, a birth, unusual visitors, bold predictions, a powerful enemy, and a daring escape. That is the human story—but every turn of events was directed by the hand of the Divine. It is really His story—the story of God and His love, and that unmistakable theme is woven throughout the narrative.

The plot was ordained at some point "in the beginning" of time. For God, in His love for fallen mankind, put the plan in place many years before the actual event. Jewish law pointed forward to a sacrificial Lamb—pure and without spot or blemish. God promised throughout the entire Old Testament that the day would finally arrive. And God always keeps His promises.

THEME

The message—sometimes overt, sometimes subtle—that the writer is attempting to convey to the reader.

The purpose of a story is to present this message as clearly and effectively as possible so the reader will understand it and, perhaps, change his or her behavior as a result of it.

Verily, verily, I say unto thee, We speak that we do know, and testify that we have seen; and ye receive not our witness. If I have told you earthly things, and ye believe not, how shall ye believe, if I tell you of heavenly things? And no man hath ascended up to heaven, but he that came down from heaven, even the Son of man which is in heaven. And as Moses lifted up the serpent in the wilderness, even so must the Son of man be lifted up: That whosoever believeth in him should not perish, but have eternal life. For God so loved the world, that he gave his only begotten Son, that whosoever believeth in him should not perish, but have everlasting life. For God sent not his Son into the world to condemn the world; but that the world through him might be saved. He that believeth on him is not condemned: but he that believeth not is condemned already, because he hath not believed in the name of the only begotten Son of God. And this is the condemnation, that light is come into the world, and men loved darkness rather than light, because their deeds were evil. For every one that doeth evil hateth the light, neither cometh to the light, lest his deeds should be reproved. But he that doeth truth cometh to the light, that his deeds may be made manifest, that they are wrought in God.

JOHN 3:11–21

THE THEME OF THE CHRISTMAS story is God's divine love for a fallen human race. His love was presented in a tiny package that arrived in Bethlehem one dark, chilly, winter's night and it was spelled out in one word: Jesus.

Jesus—a simple name with so much power and meaning, but on that night so long ago, the tiny baby, wrapped by Mary in swaddling clothes, waving little arms, hungrily sucking a fist, was like any other newborn baby. He was helpless and dependent, and Mary was His hope of survival, His nourishment, His very lifeline. God entrusted His most priceless gift to a very human, very young, earthly mother. Why? Because God so loved—that He gave. He relinquished His hold on His Son and placed Him in fragile human arms. He sent Him to minister and eventually to die. His death was no surprise to the Father. It was part of the plot and essential to the theme. There was no other way for sinners to be reconciled to a holy and just God.

THE TIME

TIME

The point in history when the story takes place.

But when the fulness of the time was come,
God sent forth his Son, made of a woman,
made under the law, To redeem them that
were under the law, that we might receive
the adoption of sons. And because ye are
sons, God hath sent forth the Spirit of his
Son into your hearts, crying, Abba, Father.
Wherefore thou art no more a servant, but
a son; and if a son, then an heir of God
through Christ.

GALATIANS 4:4-7

THE TIME IS GIVEN AS 4 OR 5 B.C. but really we understand it as the backstroke of the pendulum of God's big timepiece, for all that came before was in preparation for the event, and all that has followed looks back to the occasion. God established the Jewish laws in anticipation of the time when the Lamb of God would make the "once-and-for-all" sacrifice. After the events of Calvary, mankind would experience renewed relationship with the Father by looking back and accepting the work of the Son. "It is finished" are the words that fill the heart of every believer with joy and appreciation.

Scripture states, "When the fullness of the time was come, God sent forth his Son" (Galatians 4:4). The fullness of time—what a strange description of the world at that time. For the chosen people of God it could not have been more bleak. The once proud, powerful nation of Israel no longer was the heart of the world. Palestine served a foreign ruler. Arrogant and unscrupulous world leaders vied for position and power. Corrupt alliances, treasons, treachery, and vice were on every hand. Even many of the Jewish religious leaders had sold out to power and prosperity, which to some seemed necessary for survival. Those still clinging rigidly to the Old Testament laws tended to view them as their only hope of salvation, putting more faith in them than in the God who gave them.

Within the small country of Palestine the people were tired and depressed. They had waited "too long" for the Messiah—the Savior who would rescue them from their oppressors. Men appointed themselves as leaders and attempted to take the law into their own hands by gathering disgruntled followers into vigilante bands that tried to shake Roman rule.

Even though Roman dominance meant submission to Roman power, it did assure a measure of protection and security. And earlier Greek rule had resulted in a common language being used by many of the people from small country to small country. So people could move throughout the empire with a measure of freedom and, to some degree, converse with one another.

Simple, humble-hearted believers still were praying, watching, hoping, and waiting for the coming of the promised Messiah. Were these factors part of the reason God considered the time to be

right? Or was it that the Jewish people—
His chosen—had come to the end of their
own resources? Were they humbled and
humiliated and ready to listen to the
voice of God?

We don't know for sure, but we
believe that God chose the time for a
specific reason, and He who sees and
knows all things knew the time was right.
He planned it so.

COME, THOU LONG-EXPECTED JESUS

Come, Thou long-expected Jesus,
  Born to set Thy people free;
From our fears and sins release us;
  Let us find our rest in Thee.
Israel's Strength and Consolation,
  Hope of all the earth Thou art;
Dear Desire of every nation,
  Joy of every longing heart.
Born Thy people to deliver,
  Born a child and yet a King,
Born to reign in us forever,
  Now Thy gracious Kingdom bring.
By Thine own eternal Spirit
  Rule in all our hearts alone;
By Thine all-sufficient merit
  Raise us to Thy Glorious throne.

CHARLES WESLEY

THE SETTING

SETTING

The background for the story; the place where the action occurs.

But thou, Bethlehem Ephratah, though thou be little among the thousands of Judah, yet out of thee shall he come forth unto me that is to be ruler in Israel; whose goings forth have been from of old, from everlasting.

MICAH 5:2-3

And Joseph also went up from Galilee, out of the city of Nazareth, into Judaea, unto the city of David, which is called Bethlehem: (because he was of the house and lineage of David:) To be taxed with Mary his espoused wife, being great with child. And so it was, that, while they were there, the days were accomplished that she should be delivered. And she brought forth her firstborn son, and wrapped him in swaddling clothes, and laid him in a manger; because there was no room for them in the inn.

LUKE 2:4-7

FOR THOSE OF US LOOKING BACK IN time, the setting was the ancient world. For people of that day, however, it was the "modern" world. For those fortunate enough to be in power or favored by those who ruled, it undoubtedly seemed like an exciting, progressive time. Greek was still used as the official trade language, and though the power of the once great land of Greece had been seized by the Romans, the Greek influence was still felt. Greece had brought culture, wealth, and advancement. On the other hand, it also had fostered immorality and self-indulgence. Greek religions had left their mark on many cities, and Rome, though now totally in control, seemed quite willing to allow the people to continue their idolatrous worship—anything to keep the people happy—as long as it did not conflict with the pagan worship of the Romans themselves.

"All roads lead to Rome" was a common slogan of the day, and little insignificant lands such as Palestine had to bow the knee, if not the heart, to the mighty Roman rulers.

Palestine was only one of the small countries under Rome—a people who had been chosen of God, yet living under the oppressive heel of the great Roman Empire. A proud people, a religious people—the Israelites were unable to spring the trap that held them in insufferable bondage.

Nazareth had little of which to boast. It was situated among the southern ridges of Lebanon on the steep slope of a hill, about fourteen miles from the Sea of Galilee and about six miles from Mount Tabor. The main road between Egypt and the interior of Asia passed Nazareth at the foot of Tabor. Nazareth itself was a trading town, filled with rough and tumble tradespeople. Camel drivers and soldiers, opportunists and refugees, often stopped at Nazareth for rest and whatever safety could be found—or perhaps to gain profit from the townspeople.

Bethlehem, about eighty treacherous miles away, had reason for pride. It was from Bethlehem that King David and his line had come. It was a tiny town among the fields grazed by sheep, and the true Jews looked to it with respect. Had not their mighty king been born there? Did not the hills still echo with the bleats of his flock? Had he not led the people to the height of power and prominence? And had not the great God of Israel promised that of David's line, and in his town, a new king would one day be born? A King who would rule the world. It had been promised. Didn't that mean they would once again be powerful, wealthy, and free? How wonderful it would be to get back the dignity and respect due the chosen people of the Almighty God.

THE CHARACTERS

CHARACTERS

The people whose traits incline them to fulfill
the actions of the plot and to carry out the
theme.

He was in the world, and the world was
made by him, and the world knew him not.
He came unto his own, and his own received
him not. But as many as received him, to
them gave he power to become the sons of
God, even to them that believe on his name:
Which were born, not of blood, nor of the
will of the flesh, nor of the will of man,
but of God. And the Word was made flesh,
and dwelt among us, (and we beheld his
glory, the glory as of the only begotten of
the Father,) full of grace and truth.

JOHN 1:10–14

47

THE CHARACTERS OF THE CHRIST-
mas story are many and varied.
Good guys and bad guys, heroes and vil-
lains, the weak and the powerful, the
righteous and the self-righteous.

CAESAR

And it came to pass in those days, that
there went out a decree from Caesar
Augustus, that all the world should be
taxed. (And this taxing was first made
when Cyrenius was governor of
Syria.) And all went to be taxed, every
one into his own city.   LUKE 2:1-3

Although Caesar hadn't considered being a part of God's plan, he wound up at the very center of it. History indicates that he thought he was very much in charge of the world, and there is no evidence that the Hebrew God was of any importance in his thinking.

Luke 2 mentions him. Mentions—that is all.

His full adopted name was Gaius Julius Caesar Octavius. As the great-nephew of Julius Caesar, he used the name *Caesar* out of courtesy and by adoption. Julius Caesar, having no son of his own, named his nephew as heir in his will. Octavius was away studying when the news of Julius Caesar's death reached him, and, at only eighteen years of age, he left school and took on the responsibility of the Roman Empire. Depending on which historian you read, his reign was either virtuous or villainous.

He was very complex, and though he was not the genius his uncle had been, he was crafty. As might be expected, he had opposition—which he overcame by making treaties, by gaining political control (which often included doing away with his opponent), or by winning battles. He was the first Roman Emperor.

The name *Augustus* is significant. Caesar Augustus declined being called *dictator*, feeling it suggested a temporary office, and he didn't want to be called *king* because it signified too little. There were and had been many little kings over many little countries throughout the then-known world. So a new title was created for him—Augustus—derived from the word *Augur* and indicating not just a political but also a religious sanction. He was moving toward that which subsequently happened—the claim of deity on the part of the supreme ruler of the Roman Empire.

Gradually the power of government had been taken from the people and vested in military governors, and at last a man—an able and astute man—held all the power. The Roman Republic had passed away and in its place was the Roman Empire under Augustus Caesar.

This did not happen overnight. It was a long and often uphill pull for the new Emperor. He lived from 63 B.C. to A.D. 14 and began his struggle for power at a very young age. In 31 B.C. he finally defeated Mark Antony at Actium and from then on his rise seemed more certain.

At the time of Christ's birth the doors of the Temple of Janus had been closed for more than a decade, and they remained closed for a total of thirty years. Closed doors meant no war; when Rome was at war the doors were flung wide open.

Closed doors. No wars for thirty years. Beautiful? No. The world had been bludgeoned into submission and crushed under the heel of a merciless, tyrannical ruler. All power was vested in one man. Hegemony. World mastery. Total control by one who sought his own pleasures.

So Augustus Caesar, in all of his pomp and arrogance, decided to "poll" his people. Note Luke's words: "all the world." The ruler issued a decree that ordered all people to go to their home city to register. Luke's statement that all of the world was under one man's domination and totally at his mercy in all matters is significant. Certainly there were scatterings of humanity that Rome did not directly rule, but they were small and without political clout or power. Rome felt no concern for such little clusters of people.

The Roman coffers must have been

low—or lower than usual—and Augustus wanted to be certain that he was missing no one's tax dollars. There was no appeal, no excuse, no proxy allowed.

"And it came to pass in those days, that there went out a decree from Caesar Augustus," Luke wrote. But 650 years earlier another *decree* had been written, "But thou Bethlehem—out of thee shall come the Ruler of Israel" (Micah 5:2).

As it turned out, the really insignificant person in the drama was the puppet in the city on the seven hills—Augustus Caesar—and the really important personalities—the most important persons in the entire universe at the time—were the lowly peasant woman who was carrying God's Son and the man who was guarding her.

They went to Bethlehem because Caesar had issued a decree. Caesar issued a decree—why? Not because he was brilliant, powerful, or in total control of the then-known world. Augustus Caesar was not the "god" that he saw himself to be. God saw that it was "time"—time for the true ruler of the world to make His earthly appearance. And Bethlehem had already been established as the place where the Messiah would be born. Though Caesar was oblivious to the fact, God had chosen to use him—worldly and power-driven though he was—to accomplish His divine purpose. Caesar had no more say in the matter than the lowly Joseph had about paying the hated tax. What irony! Did God smile just a bit as He watched the blustering, pompous dictator gloat in his false sense of power?

HEROD

Then Herod, when he saw that he was mocked of the wise men, was exceeding

> wroth, and sent forth, and slew all the children that were in Bethlehem, and in all the coasts thereof, from two years old and under, according to the time which he had diligently inquired of the wise men. MATTHEW 2:16

At the same time, Herod, known as Herod the Great, was king in Palestine. Josephus says that Herod was appointed procurator of Galilee when he was fifteen but others think that the age of twenty-five might be more accurate. Herod was an Idumean—from Edomite stock, a descendant of Esau. He accepted circumcision and thus embraced the Jewish religion yet he remained heathen in practice—crafty, jealous, cruel, and vengeful. Mark Antony gave Herod a tetrarchy and afterward persuaded the Roman Senate to make Herod a king.

Herod had a passion for magnificent architecture and monuments. To reconcile the Jews who, to put it mildly, didn't care for him nor trust him, he set about reconstructing Solomon's temple. Some believe his secret motive was to get his hands on the Jewish genealogies kept there—especially the ones concerning the priestly families—to help him destroy the line before the promised Messiah could ever appear.

Augustus said of Herod, making a pun on two Greek words that sounded very much alike, that "it was better to be Herod's pig [sow] than his son," meaning that Herod would allow nothing or no one to stand in his way. History records that he ordered the death of a beloved wife because he suspected that she was disloyal. He killed his oldest son because he thought he plotted against him. He assassinated members of the Pharisees, a pious Jewish sect, because he feared them. It was in keeping with his character to vent his anger on as many persons as possible. The killing of all the male children under the age of two would seem like nothing to one who had massacred on a large scale. Tradition claims that even his own child was among those killed.

Herod—a vengeful, hateful, jealous, unreasonable, unjust tyrant, trying to protect his crown and his throne. He lived only a short time after his dreadful slaughter of the innocent.

JOSEPH

Now the birth of Jesus Christ was on

this wise: When as his mother Mary was espoused to Joseph, before they came together, she was found with child of the Holy Ghost. Then Joseph her husband, being a just man, and not willing to make her a publick example, was minded to put her away privily. But while he thought on these things, behold, the angel of the Lord appeared unto him in a dream, saying, Joseph, thou son of David, fear not to take unto thee Mary thy wife: for that which is conceived in her is of the Holy Ghost. And she shall bring forth a son, and thou shalt call his name

JESUS: for he shall save his people from their sins. Now all this was done, that it might be fulfilled which was spoken of the Lord by the prophet, saying, Behold, a virgin shall be with child, and shall bring forth a son, and they shall call his name Emmanuel, which being interpreted is, God with us. Then Joseph being raised from sleep did as the angel of the Lord had bidden him, and took unto him his wife: And knew her not till she had brought forth her firstborn son: and he called his name JESUS.

MATTHEW 1:18-25

In the faraway outpost of Palestine, the turbulent little scrap of land lying east of the Mediterranean, Augustus Caesar's edict was proclaimed as well, and all people—rich and poor, peasant and merchant, sick and well—had to go as directed.

Amid the throng of people who had to obey Caesar's decree was Joseph, a simple laborer who by this time had the care and keeping of a new wife who was soon to become a mother.

That her day for delivery was near would not have mattered to Augustus. Indeed, the lives of these lowly peasants—though the blood of King David coursed through their veins—meant nothing to the haughty ruler.

Though a descendant of Israel's royalty, Joseph was now under total subjection to Rome. How the heavy taxes must have rankled him. But Joseph was a law-abiding citizen. He was also devout and careful to attend to each demand of the religious law.

When we first meet Joseph he is betrothed, or espoused. The Jewish betrothal differed from today's engagement in that it was totally binding. A betrothal was arranged by parents or a family member or friend, and vows were taken and gifts exchanged. Sometimes a ring was presented to the bride-to-be.

Later the groom came to "take" his bride. He would arrive with his groomsmen and be met by the waiting bride and her excited maidens.

Amid music and merriment he would escort her to his or his father's house for a feast with attendants, relatives, and friends. The celebration, complete with entertainment, would last for seven to fourteen days and may well have been the first opportunity for the bride and groom to communicate with each other.

The last act of the ceremony was the conducting of the bride to the bride-chamber. Until she entered the bride-chamber she remained veiled.

Brides were often very young, some as young as ten, but the more common age was sixteen to eighteen.

For a woman to cancel the betrothal was impossible. If a man changed his mind he had to give the woman a writ or notice of divorcement and pay a fine. If the man died during the time of betrothal, the woman was considered a widow.

According to Jewish law, Joseph, in the presence of two witnesses, could have divorced Mary because of her pregnancy. She would have been publicly exposed and branded as an immoral woman. Jewish law also would have allowed that she be stoned to death.

As a good Jew, Joseph would have shown his religious zeal if he had denounced Mary. Scripture seems to indicate a short but difficult struggle between his legal conscience and his loving concern. God intervened and Joseph listened. That in itself shows Joseph's open-hearted relationship to the Father.

Mary's story would have been unbelievable to him had it not been for one fact: Joseph knew the Scriptures. He knew that God had promised a Messiah who would be born of a virgin.

Yet who would have thought that such a simple man as Joseph would be part of such a wondrous plan? He must have been awestruck by the honor and responsibility.

Scripture calls Joseph "just," and the fact that he accepted Mary in her condition and cared for her as a husband would care for his wife and coming child tells us much about Joseph.

We do not know when Joseph officially "claimed his bride" or if the traditional wedding procession took place with shouts of joy and celebration. Perhaps Joseph went alone to claim Mary, and then, silently, maybe under the cover of darkness, took her to his prepared home. Due to Mary's pregnancy, the public celebration of their marriage must have been lacking.

Did Joseph and Mary feel cheated? Shamed?

Though they lived in the same house, they did not live as husband and wife until after the birth of Jesus.

Were they able to talk to each other about their fears and feelings concerning the momentous event that was about to occur?

Or was each of them locked away in a private world, confused and perhaps frightened by the event that was about to change the whole world as well as their individual lives?

We are told little about the relationship between Joseph and Jesus—except that Jesus was "subject" to him.

God had told Joseph, through the angel Gabriel, that this child was special indeed. A lesser man might have sought some recognition for his role, but we have no reason to think that Joseph did.

Elisabeth

And Mary arose in those days, and
went into the hill country with haste,
into a city of Juda; And entered into
the house of Zacharias, and saluted
Elisabeth. And it came to pass, that,
when Elisabeth heard the salutation of
Mary, the babe leaped in her womb;
and Elisabeth was filled with the Holy
Ghost: And she spake out with a loud
voice, and said, Blessed art thou among
women, and blessed is the fruit of thy
womb. And whence is this to me, that
the mother of my Lord should come

to me? For, lo, as soon as the voice of thy salutation sounded in mine ears, the babe leaped in my womb for joy. And blessed is she that believed: for there shall be a performance of those things which were told her from the Lord. LUKE 1:39–45

What a wonderful provision of a loving God to give to the young Mary, Elisabeth.

Elisabeth was a much older woman, devout, faithful, married to a priest, and kin to Mary. She too was expecting her first child. Mary needed someone she

could talk to, someone who would understand. Mary especially needed someone
to verify that the baby she carried was
indeed as God had planned.

Mary spent three months with
Elisabeth and must have returned home
strengthened and encouraged and ready
to face the days ahead. How like God to
supply an Elisabeth.

Mary

And in the sixth month the angel Gabriel
was sent from God unto a city of Galilee, named Nazareth. To a virgin

espoused to a man whose name was Joseph, of the house of David; and the virgin's name was Mary. And the angel came in unto her, and said, Hail, thou that art highly favoured, the Lord is with thee: blessed art thou among women. And when she saw him, she was troubled at his saying, and cast in her mind what manner of salutation this should be. And the angel said unto her, Fear not, Mary: for thou hast found favour with God. And, behold, thou shalt conceive in thy womb, and bring forth a son, and shalt call his name Jesus. He shall be great, and shall be called the Son of the Highest: and the Lord God shall give unto him the throne of his father David: And he shall reign over the house of Jacob for ever; and of his kingdom there shall be no end. Then said Mary unto the angel, How shall this be, seeing I know not a man? And the angel answered and said unto her, The Holy Ghost shall come upon thee, and the power of the Highest shall overshadow thee: therefore also that holy thing which shall be born of thee shall be called the Son of God. And, behold, thy cousin Elisabeth, she hath also conceived a son in her old age: and this is the sixth month with her, who was called barren. For with God nothing shall be impossible. And Mary said, Behold the handmaid of the Lord; be it unto me according to thy word. And the angel departed from her. LUKE 1:26-38

We do not know if Mary's parents had stressed to her the great promise of God—that a Messiah would come who would deliver His people from bondage and oppression and that a special maiden would be chosen by God himself as the "virgin mother" of the child. We have nothing in Scripture to indicate that Mary was in any way prepared for the announcement of the angel. We do however have her response. First she was incredulous. "How can this be?" And when the angel explained that the Holy Child would not have an earthly father, Mary, in humility and obedience, said in essence, "Let God's will be done—His plan be accomplished. . . . Be it unto me according to thy Word."

And Mary said, My soul doth magnify the Lord, And my spirit hath rejoiced in God my Saviour. For he hath

regarded the low estate of his hand-
maiden: for, behold, from henceforth
all generations shall call me blessed.
For he that is mighty hath done to me
great things; and holy is his name. And
his mercy is on them that fear him
from generation to generation. He
hath shewed strength with his arm; he
hath scattered the proud in the imagi-
nation of their hearts. He hath put
down the mighty from their seats, and
exalted them of low degree. He hath
filled the hungry with good things;
and the rich he hath sent empty away.
He hath holpen his servant Israel, in

remembrance of his mercy; As he spake to our fathers, to Abraham, and to his seed for ever. LUKE 1:46–55

This young, sensitive, devout woman was willing to be used by God. Mary's day was not our day. It must have meant dreadful shame, humiliation, misunderstanding, and a measure of fear and wonder, but she accepted her role.

How difficult was her situation. With child, outside of the full marriage union, and joined to a man in name only. She went through the difficult time of pregnancy without the intimacies of a true husband-wife relationship, and when the event finally took place she was alone in a cold cattle shed. At the time when she was especially vulnerable and in need of the most tender care, she was on her own—as far as Scripture indicates—without even an attendant or midwife.

Though songs and pictures would have us believe that a gentle Joseph was standing by, Jewish law would have forbidden any man, even a husband, from being present at a birth.

Was her labor long and difficult, brought about by the arduous journey? Was the crude, hard-packed, earthen floor rough and cold? Did she weep for her mother?

Luke says she brought forth her firstborn son—she wrapped Him in swaddling clothes—she laid Him in a manger. Mary was the one who delivered, who cared for her own needs and those of her infant baby alone on that dark night in the distant stable—away from mother— from bed—and from home.

As she listened to the fussing of the restless village dogs and hoped with all of her heart that the stirring stable animals would not press in too closely around her and the manger, did she hope that she had remembered all the rules for the proper care of a newborn? Did she long for another visit with Elisabeth? Did she yearn for assurance that it really was as the angel had spoken? Did she wonder if she was in the middle of a bad dream from which she was unable to awaken?

Yet the baby, her baby, was so beautiful by the light of the dim lantern. How she must have longed to share with someone the joy of giving birth to her first child. But there was no one, no one with whom to share. Did she call for Joseph as soon as she had finished her simple ministrations? Were her eyes glowing, was her face flushed as she looked on the new little form lying in the crude manger-cradle? Was Joseph able to respond to the wonder of the moment? Did he feel the freedom to place his arm around Mary and draw her close as they smiled at their newborn child, tears heedlessly dampening their night-cooled cheeks?

Or did Mary have to push her feelings deep within her troubled yet joyous soul, for no one else, no one could understand the things she was feeling. She was alone. Alone.

Mary—God's chosen. Now we are

quick to praise her, but on that lonely night so long ago, it was not so. Scripture gives us hints that Mary had questions even in the time following. "Mary kept all these things and pondered them in her heart. . . . Mary marvelled at the things spoken."

What thoughts and feelings occupied the young mother? Was there a mixture of joy and shame? Of promise and doubt? Of hope and fear? What thoughts did Mary wrestle with in the days following Jesus' birth? What secret prayers did she whisper in the days that followed as she ground wheat for the daily bread or carried water from the public well, her eyes always returning to study her infant son? Was it really true? Had she, Mary, a lowly maiden, really given birth to the Son of the living God? How could it possibly be true? And if so, what lay ahead for Him? For her? For Joseph? For the world?

SHEPHERDS

And there were in the same country shepherds abiding in the field, keeping watch over their flock by night. And, lo, the angel of the Lord came upon them, and the glory of the Lord shone round about them: and they were sore afraid. And the angel said unto them, Fear not: for, behold, I bring you good tidings of great joy, which shall be to all people. For unto you is born this day in the city of David a Saviour, which is Christ the Lord. And this shall be a sign unto you; Ye shall find the babe wrapped in swaddling clothes, lying in a manger. And suddenly there was with the angel a multitude of the heavenly host praising God, and saying, Glory to God in the highest, and on earth peace, good will toward men.

And it came to pass, as the angels were gone away from them into heaven, the shepherds said one to another, Let us now go even unto Bethlehem, and see this thing which is come to pass, which the Lord hath made known unto us. And they came with haste, and found Mary, and Joseph, and the babe lying in a manger. And when they had seen it, they made known abroad the saying which was told them concerning this child. And all they that heard it wondered at those things which were told them by the shepherds. But Mary kept all these things, and pondered them in her heart. And the shepherds returned, glorifying and praising God for all the things that they had heard and seen, as it was told unto them.   LUKE 2:8-20

Shepherds were simple people, often ridiculed and sometimes even looked on with suspicion because they were unlearned, uncouth men of the land. It was not unusual for them to be in the fields by night, for shepherds often slept under the stars with their flocks. It was at night that the flock often faced the gravest danger, and the shepherds needed to be alert.

Some students of the Bible believe that the shepherds who first saw the star were the keepers of the temple flocks, those who watched over the sheep used for the daily sacrifices on the temple altar.

If so, on that starry, wintry night, they were the ideal group to be the first ones introduced to the "Lamb of God" who would take away the sins of the world. They would have understood the need for the sacrifice, the importance of the spotless lamb, and the relief from guilt that the sacrifice would accomplish.

Why did God send an angel to tell

the good news to the shepherds? We do not know, but we do know that they listened, responded, and rejoiced. They understood the message. They didn't even doubt. They left to go to see the child. The Messiah, so long promised, had come—the shepherds found Him and published the good news abroad. Were they believed? By some. It was a start.

The wise men

Now when Jesus was born in Bethlehem of Judaea in the days of Herod the king, behold, there came wise men from the east to Jerusalem, Saying, Where is he that is born King of the Jews? for we have seen his star in the east, and are come to worship him. When Herod the king had heard these things, he was troubled, and all Jerusalem with him. And when he had gathered all the chief priests and scribes of the people together, he demanded of them where Christ should be born. And they said unto him, In Bethlehem of Judaea: for thus it is written by the prophet, And thou Bethlehem, in the land of Juda, art not the least among the princes of Juda: for out of thee shall come a Governor, that shall rule my people Israel. Then Herod, when he had privily called the wise men, inquired of them diligently what time the star appeared. And he sent them to Bethlehem, and said, Go and search diligently for the young child; and when ye have found him, bring me word again, that I may come and worship him also. When they had heard the king, they departed; and, lo, the star, which they saw in the east, went before them, till it came and stood over where the young child was. When they saw the star, they rejoiced with exceeding great joy. And when they were come into the house, they saw the young child with Mary his mother, and fell down, and worshipped him: and when they had opened their treasures, they presented unto him gifts; gold, and frankincense, and myrrh. And being warned of God in a dream that they should not return to Herod, they departed into their own country another way. MATTHEW 2:1-12

The Greek word used to describe the Magi means "wise man and priest who was expert in astrology, interpretation of dreams, and various other arts."

The East might refer to Arabia, as some have concluded by the nature of the gifts, or to Babylonia, the home of astrology. Tradition holds them to be kings, and the three gifts mentioned have led to the conclusion that there were three of them. Whoever they were, and from wherever they came, they came with one purpose—to worship.

By now the Christ child was no longer in the manger. Scripture says that when they "had come into the house" they worshiped Him. How much time had elapsed? We do not know. Months? Perhaps. A year? More? Perhaps nearly two years. After finding out when the star had first appeared, Herod, "just to be sure," searched out all the baby boys two years of age and younger and had them murdered to prevent the one "born King of the Jews" from rising to power and usurping his throne.

How long had the wise men been following the star? Scripture does not say, but it implies their journey was a lengthy one. Imagine embarking on such a long and costly journey simply to spend a few minutes worshiping at the feet of a lowly child. What had they to gain? Was it worth the sacrifice? Scripture gives no hint that the wise men felt cheated. They followed the star of promise, found the child, fell down before Him, worshiped Him, presented their costly gifts, and protected the young child by returning home secretly. A long, arduous journey just to worship a young child.

But not just a young child—a new and unusual King.

THE RELIGIOUS LEADERS

When Herod the king had heard these things, he was troubled, and all Jerusalem with him. And when he had gathered all the chief priests and scribes of the people together, he demanded of them where Christ should be born. And they said unto him, In Bethlehem of Judaea: for thus it is written by the prophet, And thou Bethlehem, in the land of Juda, art not the least among the princes of Juda: for out of thee shall come a Governor, that shall rule my people Israel.

MATTHEW 2:3-6

The religious leaders of the day supposedly knew the Scriptures well and were waiting for the coming of the promised

Messiah. When questioned, they imme-
diately were able to tell Herod the birth-
place of the promised King of the Jews.
They even quoted the Old Testament
words and references, but there is no
indication that they themselves made an
effort to find the Messiah.

There is only one short commen-
tary. When asked what Scripture said
concerning His birth, they knew the
answer.

How sad that it made such little
impact on the chief priest and scribes.
How sad when the truth is available but
the heart has no desire to respond.

THE CENTRAL FIGURE

And, behold, there was a man in Jerusalem, whose name was Simeon; and
the same man was just and devout,
waiting for the consolation of Israel:
and the Holy Ghost was upon him.
And it was revealed unto him by the
Holy Ghost, that he should not see
death, before he had seen the Lord's
Christ. And he came by the Spirit into
the temple: and when the parents
brought in the child Jesus, to do for
him after the custom of the law, Then
took he him up in his arms, and blessed

God, and said, Lord, now lettest thou
thy servant depart in peace, according
to thy word: For mine eyes have seen
thy salvation, Which thou hast prepared before the face of all people; A
light to lighten the Gentiles, and the
glory of thy people Israel. And Joseph
and his mother marvelled at those
things which were spoken of him. And
Simeon blessed them, and said unto
Mary his mother, Behold, this child is
set for the fall and rising again of many
in Israel; and for a sign which shall be
spoken against; (Yea, a sword shall
pierce through thy own soul also,) that

the thoughts of many hearts may be
revealed.   LUKE 2:25-35

"You shall call Him Jesus." Jesus was a
common name for sons in Mary's day. It
was the Greek form of the Hebrew
Joshua—meaning Savior. Many mothers
named their sons Joshua in the hope that
they would grow up to "save Israel" from
bondage. But the angel who brought the
announcement brought also an added
promise. He shall save His people not
from Roman rule, not from political
bondage, and not from financial or phys-
ical oppression—but from "their sin."

Jesus—the Bethlehem baby. Bundled against the chill of a winter night by a very young mother. Jesus—accepted by Joseph as his charge. Jesus—visited and praised by lowly shepherds. Jesus—worshiped by wise men who traveled far to lay their costly gifts at His tiny feet. Jesus—an infant feared by a mad king. Jesus—unrecognized as a possibility and a promise by most of the religious leaders of the day. Jesus—whose life and death have changed history—who can dwell with us and in us as our Savior, Lord, and King. Jesus—the ever-present God who frees us from the bondage of sin—a bondage more real and more devastating and more permanent than the bondage of Roman rule. Jesus—the tiny Bethlehem baby—yet a name that encompasses beauty and grace, hope and power. For we cannot think of the name without thinking beyond to a hill on Mount Calvary—and even beyond that to an empty tomb and His resurrection promise, "Lo, I am with you alway."

Jesus

How sweet the name
of Jesus sounds

How sweet the name of Jesus sounds
  In a believer's ear!
It soothes his sorrows, heals his wounds,
  And drives away his fear.
It makes the wounded spirit whole
  And calms the troubled breast;
'Tis nourishment to hungry souls,
  And to the weary rest.
Jesus! my Savior, Shepherd, Friend,
  My Prophet, Priest, and King,
My Lord, my Life, my Way, my End,
  Accept the praise I bring.
Weak is the effort of my heart,
  And cold my warmest thought;
But when I see Thee as Thou art,
  I'll praise Thee as I ought.

JOHN NEWTON

THE $\mathcal{C}$LIMAX

Climax

The highest point in a series of events of ascending intensity (Webster). The final event for which the whole process was designed.

For this we say unto you by the word of the Lord, that we which are alive and remain unto the coming of the Lord shall not prevent them which are asleep. For the Lord himself shall descend from heaven with a shout, with the voice of the archangel, and with the trump of God: and the dead in Christ shall rise first: Then we which are alive and remain shall be caught up together with them in the clouds, to meet the Lord in the air: and so shall we ever be with the Lord. Wherefore comfort one another with these words.

1 THESSALONIANS 4:15–18

THE CLIMAX OF THE CHRISTMAS story might at first be thought to be the birth of the baby or the escape from Herod. But the ultimate climax is yet to come.

The Bridegroom is about to claim His cherished Bride. The betrothal has been arranged, the dowry paid, the promise given, and the home is being prepared. The next step will be the Bridegroom's journey to claim what is already His—the Church, His Bride. And the waiting Bride must be ready to join her Bridegroom at the wedding. The Feast will follow, as the Bride, redeemed by her Bridegroom and dressed in glimmering garments of white, is presented to the Father and to the hosts of Heaven.

May it be an event of tremendous celebration and great rejoicing—not just for Him, but for me and for you as well.

This is the Christmas story—
the greatest love story of all time.